Stripes and Spots

by Ruth Mattison

Pioneer Valley Educational Press, Inc.

Here is a zebra.
The zebra has stripes.
The zebra can hide
in the grass.

Here is a tiger.

The tiger has stripes.

The tiger can hide
in the grass, too.

Here is a frog.
The frog has spots.
The frog can hide
in the pond.

Here is a baby cheetah.
Look at the spots
on the cheetah.
The cheetah can hide
in the grass.

Here is a fawn.
Look at the spots
on the fawn.
The fawn can hide
in the grass, too.

cheetah

fawn

frog

tiger

zebra